Group Projects

Precious McKenzie

rourkeeducationalmedia.com

Before Reading:

Building Academic Vocabulary and Background Knowledge

Before reading a book, it is important to tap into what your child or students already know about the topic. This will help them develop their vocabulary, increase their reading comprehension, and make connections across the curriculum.

1. *Look at the cover of the book. What will this book be about?*
2. *What do you already know about the topic?*
3. *Let's study the Table of Contents. What will you learn about in the book's chapters?*
4. *What would you like to learn about this topic? Do you think you might learn about it from this book? Why or why not?*
5. *Use a reading journal to write about your knowledge of this topic. Record what you already know about the topic and what you hope to learn about the topic.*
6. *Read the book.*
7. *In your reading journal, record what you learned about the topic and your response to the book.*
8. *After reading the book complete the activities below.*

Content Area Vocabulary
Read the list. What do these words mean?

effective
guidelines
management
nonverbal
opportunity
personalities
respect
strategy
stress
struggling
supervisors
teamwork

After Reading:

Comprehension and Extension Activity

After reading the book, work on the following questions with your child or students in order to check their level of reading comprehension and content mastery.

1. *What skills can be learned through group projects? (Summarize)*
2. *Why should each group member do an equal amount of work? (Infer)*
3. *How would you work with an uncooperative group member? (Text to self connection)*
4. *How does a group ensure they meet the assignment due date? (Summarize)*
5. *Describe an effective group leader. (Visualize)*

Extension Activity

After reading the book, ask a few friends to work with you on designing a new board game. You will have to create a board and pieces, make up the rules, and test the game to be sure that it works and is fun. You may have to revise the game if your test goes poorly. Follow the guidance in the text when assigning jobs, making a schedule, and holding group meetings.

Table of Contents

What Do Employers Want?

What career would you like to have when you are older? Do you want to be a veterinarian, a computer programmer, a musician, or an engineer? There is one common skill that all careers require. Do you know what that skill is? It's **teamwork**.

Teamwork is the ability to work well with other people. Good team members **respect** one another and listen to one another. They cooperate to solve problems and get the job done.

Team members value one another. They share their knowledge and talents to contribute to the success of a project.

Supervisors at companies are always looking for talented individuals who can work well with others. Why? If people can work together to get projects completed on time, this saves businesses time and money. Great team members help companies make money and provide excellent customer service. Everyone wins with teamwork!

Many skilled team members work together to deliver the best products to customers. When you visit a restaurant, think about how many people worked together to bring the food to your table. From the farmers, the chef and assistants, the host, and the server, they all worked together on a special project: your dinner!

How do you develop your teamwork skills so you can land your dream job someday? When your teacher assigns a group project in school, think of the project as the perfect **opportunity** to build your teamwork skills.

Getting Started

Group projects can be challenging and fun. You have the chance to share your talents with others. You will have the chance to learn from others, too. How do you get started with your group project?

Your teacher will give you a list of **guidelines** for your group project. Be sure to follow those guidelines closely. When you understand what your teacher wants from the project, meet with your group to come up with an action plan.

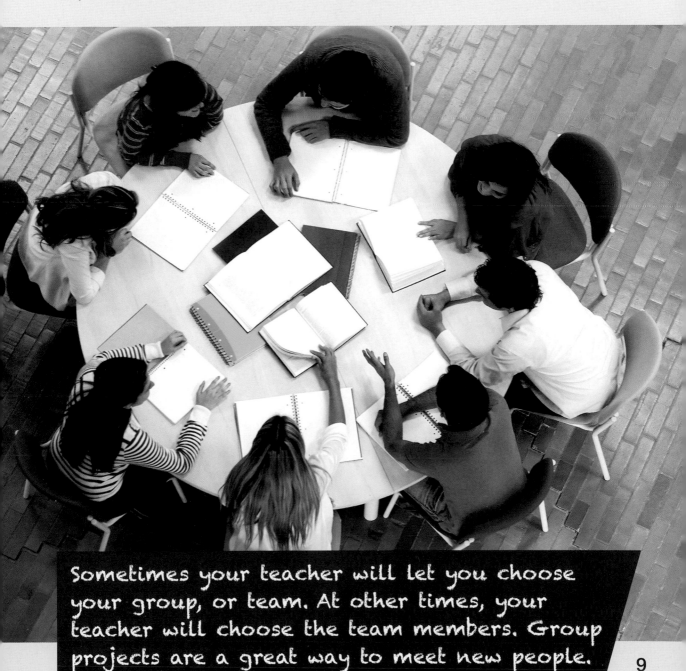

Sometimes your teacher will let you choose your group, or team. At other times, your teacher will choose the team members. Group projects are a great way to meet new people.

Group projects are usually large, complex assignments. There can be many components, or parts, to the project. A good **strategy** is to divide the project into smaller parts, called chunks. As a group, decide who will work on each chunk of the project.

Everyone is Good at Something!

Business experts recommend that group members play to one another's strengths. That means if someone in your group is a talented artist, let that person do the art or graphics for the project. If someone is a talented writer, allow that person to write the report. If a group member likes to talk and share ideas, let that person present the project to the class. With a group project, there is a job for everyone.

Be sure to divide the assignments fairly. One person should not have to do all the work. Help each other so that your group can create a fantastic project. After all, many hands make light work.

Teamwork Tips

Working with people is fun and challenging because there are many different types of **personalities**. Some people are outgoing. Some people are shy. Some students like to get their work done early while other students wait until the last minute to finish an assignment. These different personalities and work habits can create **stress** for a group.

People sometimes argue and make situations worse. Listening to one another can help solve problems and reduce stress during a group project. Talk about your problems and look for ways to help solve problems, without hurting the group or the project.

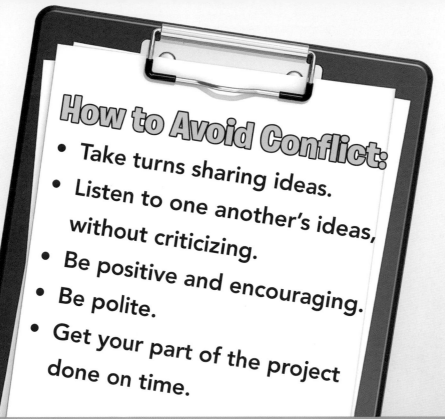

How to Avoid Conflict:

- Take turns sharing ideas.
- Listen to one another's ideas, without criticizing.
- Be positive and encouraging.
- Be polite.
- Get your part of the project done on time.

13

Nonverbal cues will let you know how your group members are doing. Pay attention to how your group members feel. Do they look happy? Are they participating and enjoying the project? Is the project moving along on time? If you answered "yes" to these questions, congratulations! Your group is doing great!

Tips for Taking a Leadership Role:

- Be positive.
- Pay attention to the verbal and nonverbal signals from your group members.
- Keep the group project on schedule and organized.
- Ask each group member to share their ideas.
- Think about what your group will need and help them get it.

Do your group members look sad? Are they quiet and not participating? Are they not completing their part of the project? If you answered "yes" to these questions, that's a sign that your group might not be working well. Be a leader and help your group! Keep a positive attitude.

Everyone wants to feel important and valuable. **Effective** group leaders keep a project on schedule and make sure group members feel valued.

Let's face it, sometimes a group will struggle to complete the project. The task may be very complex or group members may not understand the project. Maybe someone is not doing his or her part of the project. Perhaps you or your group leader tried to solve the problem but nothing worked. You can't just quit the project. What would happen to your grade? Where can you turn for help?

Questions to Ask Your Group Members:

- Is everyone doing okay?
- Is everyone enjoying the project?
- Does anyone need extra help on his or her chunk of the project?

If you've tried to solve your problem and it didn't get better, it is time to ask for help. Your teacher is a great person to turn to for help. No one knows the assignment better than your teacher. Your teacher also knows all your group members, and their personalities. Ask your teacher for advice to resolve conflict and help your group project stay on track.

If you are **struggling** with the assignment, your parents might be able to help. They can help you find extra time to meet with your group. They can take you to study sessions or to the library.

You can host a study session at your house. It will give your group a chance to get to know each other, have fun, and get the project done!

Time Management

Another challenge of a group project is time **management**. The group project is probably very large. Your teacher has assigned a due date to allow your group enough time to get the project done.

Your teacher may allow time to work on the project in class. However, you may need to work on the project after school or on the weekends as well. It can be quite a challenge to juggle group members' busy schedules. But, with some planning, you can do it!

By breaking the project into smaller chunks you will know which parts need to be completed first and which parts can be done at a later time. For example, you can't proofread the project until someone has actually written it. Work with one another to assign due dates for the chunks. Then be sure to get your chunk done on time and to the very best of your ability.

Activity: Set Up A Schedule:

- Decide on the chunks of the project.
- Assign different chunks to each group member.
- Set a schedule for each chunk. Will it take 15 minutes? A day? Four days?
- Build in a time cushion at the end of the project in case of emergencies.
- Work on your chunk of the project.
- Check in with your group to make sure everything is going okay.
- Turn your chunk in to the group on the scheduled day.
- Ask for feedback from all group members.
- Revise your work according to the group's suggestions.
- Compile your project with your group.
- Turn it in to your teacher as scheduled.

With a positive attitude and proper planning, your group project is sure to be a success.

Glossary

effective (uh-FEK-tiv): getting a job done well

guidelines (GIDE-LINEZ): rules for an assignment

management (MAN-ij-muhnt): the organization or use of something, such as time

nonverbal (non-VUR-buhl): not using words to communicate

opportunity (op-ur-TOO-nuh-tee): a good chance to do something

personalities (pur-suh-NAL-it-teez): qualities that make people different from one another

respect (ri-SPEKT): to treat someone with care and consideration

strategy (STRAT-uh-jee): a plan to help you reach your goal

stress (STRESS): worry or pressure

struggling (STRUHG-uhl-ing): trying very hard to do something

supervisors (SOO-pur-vye-zurz): people who are in charge and who lead a business

teamwork (teem-WURK): to work together to accomplish a goal

Index

Websites to Visit

http://kidshealth.org/kid/feeling/school/group_projects.html#

http://youth.usab.com/training-room/player-psychology/5-steps-to-being-a-great-leader.htm

http://www.ncld.org/students-disabilities/homework-study-skills

About the Author

Precious McKenzie lives in Billings, Montana. She teaches college students how to work on teams so they can find terrific careers after they graduate. In her free time, she likes to read books and ride horses.

Meet The Author!
www.meetREMauthors.com

© 2015 Rourke Educational Media

www.rourkeeducationalmedia.com

PHOTO CREDITS: Cover © Christopher Futcher; Title Page © Robert Kneschke; page 3 © Rido; page 5, 9, 16, 16 © Andresr, Andrey Armyagov; page 6 © auremar; page 7 © Maridav; page 8 © michaeljung; page 10 © Brian A. Jackson; page 11 © Rawpixel; page 13, 14, 17, 21 © Jojje, marcoventuriniautieri; page 15 © gpointstudio; page 16 © Konstantin chagin; page 18 © Monkey Business Images; page 19 © OtnaYdur; page 20 © Eviakhov Valeriy

Edited by: Jill Sherman

Cover Design by: Jen Thomas

Interior Design by: Rhea Magaro

Library of Congress PCN Data

Group Projects / Precious McKenzie
(Hitting the Books: Skills for Reading, Writing, and Research)
ISBN (hard cover) (alk. paper) 978-1-62717-691-0
ISBN (soft cover) 978-1-62717-813-6
ISBN (e-Book) 978-1-62717-928-7
Library of Congress Control Number: 2014935485

Rourke Educational Media
Printed in the United States of America,
North Mankato, Minnesota

Also Available as: